How to Improve Your Leadership and Management Skills

Effective Strategies for Business Managers

MEIR LIRAZ

Published by BizMove
www.bizmove.com

Table of Contents

1. How to Lead and Manage People

In organizations we must work with and for others. To be able to mutually achieve our goals we must be able to relate to others effectively. These Effective Leadership Skills Training tips will help you do just that.

- Catch people doing things right and then let them know that they are doing things right.
- Use feedback to stay informed about what other people are doing in your area of responsibility and authority.
- Have regular, focused meetings regarding the projects that you are responsible for.
- Provide adequate instructions. Time is lost if things are not done correctly.
- Train others to do jobs. You cannot do them all, nor can others do them if they have not been trained.
- Expect others to succeed. It becomes a self-fulfilling prophecy when you believe others are loyal, dedicated and doing a good job.
- Help others see how they will benefit from doing a job. This is when they truly become motivated.
- Do not avoid talking to a poor performer. It hurts them, the organization and yourself if the situation is not dealt with.
- Do not over control others. It is frustrating for them and time consuming for you.
- Focus on results, not on activities or personalities.
- Reward people for the results that they produce.
- Manage by walking around. See what people are doing and listen to what they have to say.
- Make quality an obsession, especially on smaller items.

- Send thank you notes and memos.
- Provide workers with open, direct, and immediate feedback on their actual performance as compared to expected performance and they tend to correct their own deficiencies.
- Practice naive listening. Don't talk, just let people explain why they are doing the types of things that they are doing. You will learn many things.
  Manage by exception. When things are going well, leave them alone. When a problem occurs, then help.
- Never seek to place blame. Always focus on the problem.
- Never ignore a concern of one of your people. While it may seem trivial to you, to the other person it is a problem that will continue to destroy their train of thought.
- Make it a personal rule and a challenge to respond to someone within 24 hours of hearing their request.
- Keep memos on bulletin boards to a minimum. People will spend less time standing there reading.
- Give employees an opportunity to speak their opinions and suggestions without fear of ridicule or reprisal.
- When you are going to make a change that affects others, get them involved before making the actual change. This increases commitment to make the change work after it is implemented.
- Put key ideas on small posters to hang around the office.
- When the environment and your sincerity permit, give the person a hug or a touch.
- Employees are the only organization resource that can, with training, appreciate in value. All other resources depreciate.

- People want to be involved in something important. Give them a whole project or a significant piece of the project to work on.
- Have salary tied into performance appraisal and accomplishing of objectives.
- Consider sharing distasteful tasks to reduce resentment and hard feelings.
- Ask, "Will you please do this for me" instead of telling someone just to do it.
- Eliminate private secretaries in favor of shared secretaries in order to make it easier to even out the work load.
- If you give employees a basic employee handbook, you will not be interrupted with their questions.
- Pay attention to small details, the big ones are obvious and get taken care of.
- Stay open in your thinking. Be open to all new ideas. Do this and you will not be setting up barriers that do not exist.
- Avoid asking others to do trivial personal items for you. Say thank you to those with whom you associate.
  A warm smile and strong handshake break barriers.
- Smile. It helps you feel better and is contagious. The whole organization shudders when the boss is frowning. Likewise it smiles when the boss does.
- Keep things "light" and have fun rather than being too serious. Seriousness blocks productivity.
- In order to fly with the eagles you must "think lightly."
- Work with each person to create standard operating procedures for their specific job. It will eliminate repetitious questions.
- Let people know why they are doing something. It then becomes more meaningful when they recognize their part in a greater vision.

- Provide soft, lively background music not slow and not rock.
- To get a disorganized coffee drinking crew started off more efficiently, begin each day with a 5 to 10 minute meeting just at starting time. They will be focused, set in the right direction and can get right to work.
- Practice the golden rule in business: Do unto others the way you would have them do unto you. Fairness will then be in your business.
- Practice the platinum rule in interpersonal relationships. It is "Do unto others, the way they want to be done unto." They will be more apt to stay comfortable when interacting with us when we are able to do things their preferred way.
- Get others to commit to deadlines by asking, "When can you have that for me?"
- Nail down commitment by asking, "Do I have your word that you will have that for me then?"
- Set the stage for cooperation from others by: 1) Introducing the idea; 2) Continual stimulation by talking about it; and 3) get others to make an investment by having them participate in the planning.
- If you are unable to reach agreement or get a commitment from another person in a meeting, agree to disagree, but summarize your understanding in a confirming memo.
- Giving people recognition generates energy within them. They will then direct that energy toward increased productivity.
- Tap the potential of those working for you by giving them opportunities to think things through for themselves instead of just telling them how to do something.

- Always give people the benefit of the doubt. They may not be the cause of a problem. The cause may be beyond their control.
- Admit it when you do not know the answer to a question posed by a staff member. Then challenge the staff person to research and decide what the best answer is. It will help this person grow.
- Be persistent and follow up.
- When you were away and some of your people did an exceptional job, call them at home in the evening when you find out and personally thank them for what they did instead of waiting until the next time you see them.
- If you know that a person will respond angrily to a particular comment, avoid bringing it up. It is nonproductive and bad for the relationship. In other words, "never kick a skunk."
- When you appreciate what someone has done, let them know and put it in writing. This can then be added to their personnel file.
- Have an opinion survey done to determine how people view the organization. That way you can catch any problems while they are still small.
- Encourage periods of uninterrupted activity such as a daily quiet hour in your department or work group.
- When asking someone to do something, let them know what is in it for them and the organization. Do not focus just on what is in it for the organization and yourself.
- The boss is the strongest model the employees have. Be a positive model as people are watching to see how you behave. They will reflect this in their own behavior. Lead by example.
- Be a member of the 4 F club with others. Be seen as Fair, Firm, Friendly and having Foresight.

- Do not help others unless they need and ask for help.
- Encourage your people to come up with new ideas and ways to do things. Give them credit and recognition for the idea.
- If a new idea won't work, at least praise the effort of the person so they will come up with future ideas.
- Once a month meet with each staff member to catch any problems or concerns the person may have as soon as possible before they become a crisis.
- Be the kind of a person that others want to help out and work for.
- Be flexible and do whatever it takes to get the job done. Remember it is results that count, not activities.
- Generally speaking, getting something done perfectly is usually not as important as getting it done. Perfection has a high cost and it may not be worth it.
- When giving or receiving information, don't hurry. Take the time needed to truly understand. It prevents future problems and misunderstandings.
- Whenever you are having an important discussion with a person, before parting, set a specific follow-up date and time and write it in your calendar.
- Never criticize an employee in front of others. Have all discussions of a corrective nature in private.
- Hire people with specific skills and interests that match what the organization needs to have accomplished. The better the match, the better the productivity and the more motivated the person.
- Treat people as people-not things.
- Flaring in anger will drive others away. If not physically at least mentally,
- Keep a "warm fuzzy" file for each person a place to keep track of the things you have already complimented them for, and want to compliment them for.

- Have regular performance review and goal setting sessions with each of your employees at least every three months.
- Have regular "development discussions" with each of your people in which you discuss only how the individual may grow personally and how you and the organization may be able to support them in doing this.
- Low morale in workers may be an indication of the boss only talking about negative things or what's wrong. Be sure to balance negative comments with more frequent positive comments.
- Let your people know you are there to help them not to harass them.
- Telling people what you plan to do, and when, can be a catalyst for getting objections and input which you might not otherwise receive.
- Form an action team to address people's problems right away rather than letting things drag out and perhaps get worse.
- Instead of saying to another, "What can I do for you?" ask them "What can you do for me on this project?"
- Do not hold back from discussing the need to improve performance with one of your people.
- Encourage others to develop their plan of action and give you a detailed explanation.
- Encourage individuals to compete against themselves to achieve more. Let it be a personal challenge to become better as an individual-not competing with others but self.
- Check the ratio of positive comments to negative comments that you make to your people. Purposely make more positive comments.
- Demand accountability.

- Do things for others. They will be more willing to do things for you.
- Consider using time off as a reward for getting things done ahead of time.
- Set up an orientation training program for all new employees. It will help them learn their way around as well as teach them where things are kept and why.
- Stay informed of subordinates' needs and interests. Projects can be more effectively designed and rotated when you are well informed.
- If individuals needs some encouragement in taking action, ask them, "What if..." questions to help them see what choices of action are available.
- Let people know that you know they can do it.
- Ask questions creatively so the action to be taken is suggested by the person who is to take it.
- Set up incentives that reward desired performance.
- Ask others for their estimate of how long it will take to do a project. When possible, agree and hold them accountable for that goal.
- Take on someone else's routine so they can do what you need done without interruption.
- Just as with family members, break large chores up into small, fun activities and enjoy doing them with team members.
- Before an employee leaves on vacation agree on a "must do" list of activities to be completed.
- Do not be quick to judge others. Learn to listen carefully before coming to conclusions.
- Consider sharing ideas and responsibility with others rather than just getting someone to do it for you or just doing it yourself.
- Inspire others to new levels of achievement by using positive encouraging feedback and ideas.

- Don't just ask someone who is busy to get things done for you; look for the busy person who is getting results. This is a doer, not simply a busy wheel spinner.
- Believe in the good of people.
- Do not be a "baby sitter" of others, constantly taking care of them and telling them what to do. Challenge them and help them learn to think and do things for themselves.
- Consider an incentive plan to reward productivity gains.
- Don't do what you can get someone else to do by simply asking.
- Clearly communicate who you want to do what, by when and at what cost. Then identify who needs to know about it and when they are to be informed.
- For people you relate to regularly, keep a list of things you need to talk to the person about. Then when you meet with or call them, you can review all the items that have accumulated on your list.
- Recognize you are not the only one who can do a job right. Trust others to do things for you.
- Organize, deputize, supervise.
- Meditate for one minute before starting a new subject or project.
- Don't worry about who gets the credit for completing a project. Focus on the task to be accomplished and do it.
- When credit is given to you for completion of a project, be sure to give it to all who were involved. This will nurture the relationships and provide motivation to support you in the future.
- Be sincerely interested in the people working for and with you.
- Help others recognize their own importance.
- Keep a list of birthdays, marriage and work anniversaries and other special dates. Provide

recognition to your people on each of these dates. Mark your calendar prior to the actual date so you have time to prepare for it.

2. How to Make a Good First Impression

We sometimes get only one chance to make an impression on someone either in our personal or business life. Therefore it is important to remember some basic things to do that will assure us of making the best impression possible. The following are ten of the most common things people can do to make the best first impression possible.

1. **Appear Neat And Dress Appropriately.**

Being neat in our appearance is something we can do regardless of whether we are trying to make a good impression on someone or not. In a *first meeting* situation for business, to show up in jeans, tennis shoes and with uncombed hair would be a big mistake. If the situation is social, dressing casual is fine depending on where you are meeting, but being well groomed is always going to make a good impression.

2. **Maintain Good Eye Contact.**

From the first time you meet the person until you part, maintain good direct eye contact with them. This usually indicates to people that you are listening to them, interested in them, and friendly. You need not stare or glare at them. Simply focus on them and their immediate direction the majority of the time. When talking, look at them also, since your new acquaintance wants to be sure you are talking to him/her and not the floor. It also will give you an idea of how the person is receiving what you are saying to them if you are looking at them.

3. **Shake Their Hand At The Beginning And When Parting.**

Whether it is a business meeting or a social occasion, most people appreciate or expect a friendly handshake. The best kind are firm (no need to prove your strength) and 3-5 seconds long. Pumping up and down or jerking their arm about is not needed nor usually welcomed. A *limp rag* handshake is not recommended unless you have good reason to believe shaking the person's hand any harder would injure them. Look at them in the eye when shaking their hand.

4. SMILE! :-)

A smile goes a long way in making a first impression. When you shake hands with the person, smile as you introduce yourself or say hello. Even if the other person does not smile, you can, and it will be remembered by the other person. As you talk or listen to the person speak, smile off and on to show your interest, amusement, or just to show you are being friendly.

5. Listen More Than You Talk.

Unless you are asked for your life story (in which case give a very abbreviated version) let the other person do most of the talking as you listen. Listening to your new acquaintance will give you information to refer to later, and it will give your new friend the impression you are genuinely interested in them, their business, etc. If you are asked questions, feel free to talk. If you are really bored, avoid 3-5 word sentence replies to your companion's questions. Pretend at least to be interested. You won't/don't necessarily ever have to talk with this person again.

6. Relax And Be Yourself.

Who else would you be? Well, sometimes people try to act differently than they normally would to impress or show off to a new acquaintance. Putting on facades and *airs* is not recommended, as a discerning person will sense it and it will have a negative effect on how they view you. Just be yourself and relax and *go with the flow* of conversation.

7. Ask Them About *Their* Business And Personal Life.

Show that you have an active interest in the other person's professional and personal life. When an appropriate time comes, ask them to tell you about their family and their business if they have not already done so. People love to talk about themselves. They usually feel flattered and respected when others, especially people who have never met them, show real interest in their business and their personal life. It also shows that you are not self-centered when you do not spend a lot of time talking about yourself and *your* life.

8. Don't *Name Drop* Or Brag.

Very few people you will meet for the first time will be favorably impressed if you start telling them you know Donald Trump, Don Johnson, or the CEO of Widgets, Inc. They want to get to know you and have you get to know them. Experienced and secure business people are not impressed by who you know as much as what you know. If someone asks you if you know *so and so*, then it's appropriate to tell them the truth. Unless they do, it sounds like you are very insecure and trying to really *impress them*. Bragging about your financial, business or social coups or feats is likewise in bad taste and not recommended. Just keep it simple and factual and be yourself.

9. Don't Eat Or *Drink* Too Much.

If your first meeting is at a function or place where food and alcohol are served, it is wise to eat and drink in moderation. This is especial true of drinking alcohol! You want to be able to listen well and remember what is said, and speak well for yourself. There is probably nothing that leaves a worse first impression on a business or social date than for their new *acquaintance* to get intoxicated and to say or do things that are embarrassing, rude, crude, or all three. Use good self control and eat as your new friend does, and drink only in social moderation or not at all. What is done one night under the influence of alcoholic merriment might be regretted for hundreds of nights in clear headed sobriety!

10. Part With A Smile, A Handshake And A Sincere Comment Or Compliment.

Regardless of how you felt the evening went it is simply common courtesy to shake hands when the evening is over, offer a smile and some sort of friendly comment or compliment. If it was a social evening and you had a great time, offer a sincere compliment and let them know you'd like to meet again. If it was a business meeting, offer a smile and a sincere comment around how it was nice to meet them, get to know them, learn about their business etc. You may never have to see the person again, but they may know people who they will tell about their meeting with you who you *will* work with or need to meet down the road. It always pays to be kind and polite even if you were not treated that way or did not enjoy the time you spent with someone.

3. How to Motivate Employees in the Workplace

Supervising people involves more than telling them what to do. Effective supervision involves motivation from within the individual, not by externals.

1. Treat them as individuals, not merely as necessary cogs in a wheel. Remember their personal problems, find appropriate times to ask how they or their families are, how the big event went, whether the plumbing problem got fixed.

2. Acknowledge their contributions. Let them be confident that when you pass their suggestions and contributions up the chain of command you will acknowledge the members of your team as the source.

3. Back them up. When things go wrong, the buck stops at your desk. Do not deal with problems by telling your superiors how awful your supervisees are. Tell how you will go about preventing a re-occurrence.

4. Take time for them. When a supervisee comes to you, stop what you are doing, make eye contact. If you can't be interrupted, immediately set up a later time when you will be able to pay full attention to them. Otherwise people may feel that they are bothersome to you, and you may someday find yourself wondering why no one tells you what is happening in your own department.

5. Let them know that you see their potential and encourage their growth. Encourage learning. Help them to take on extra responsibility, but be available to offer support when they are in unfamiliar territory.

6. Explain why. Provide the information that will give both purpose to their activities and understanding of your requirements. Providing information only on a need-to-know basis may work for the CIA, but it does not build teams.

7. Don't micro-manage. Let them know the plans and the goals, that you trust them to do their best, and then let them have the freedom to make at least some of the decisions as to how to do what is needed. Morale and creativity nosedive when the flow of work is interrupted by a supervisor checking on progress every two minutes.

8. Let them work to their strengths. We all like to feel good about our work. If we can do something that we do well, we will feel proud. If you believe supervisees need to strengthen areas of weakness, have them work on these, too, but not exclusively.

9. Praise in public, correct in private. NOTHING undermines morale as effectively as public humiliation.

10. Set reasonable boundaries, and empower your supervisees to set theirs. Once set, respect them. This is not a challenge to your power, it is their right as human beings.

4. How to Manage Change Effectively

1. Start with the end in mind.

We know that navigating successfully in a world that is changing as fast as ours can be tricky at times. In fact, if we allow it to overwhelm us, change can feel extremely stressful and downright frustrating. If we're smart, however, we've learned that although we can't alter the fact of constant change, we can learn to manage our response to it. Here's a sample of how I coach my clients on managing change in their lives:

1. Accept change as a fact of life.

As human beings we are constantly in process. We never get there, our in-box is never empty, and we can't catch up with technology. Our world is changing at a pace never experienced before, indeed, change is our only constant .accept it!

2. Commit yourself to lifelong learning.

If change is constant, then learning must also be continual. As long as we are learning we're on the road to an exciting, fulfilling, meaningful life. Learning helps us feel as though we're moving with the ever-changing world. This helps to relieve our anxiety of feeling left behind. We feel better because when we're learning we are moving with the world.

3. Get healthy then stay healthy

Change, even positive change, is stressful. To keep stress from getting us, we must stay physically healthy with proper nutrition, enough rest and regular exercise.

4. Look at change as an opportunity.

Changing our attitude about change is one of our best management tools. Look for opportunities in every change in your life. Rather than digging in your heels and resisting change, allow yourself to flow with it and see where it takes you.

5. Develop and maintain a strong network and support team.

Many changes in our lives require us to lean on others for emotional support and/or advice. Have your team in place ready to see you through the inevitable significant changes in your life.

6. Develop your spirituality.

God is the only aspect of our lives that is constant. She is the same today, tomorrow, and into infinity. This is a comforting and stabilizing thought in today's world. To have a friend, a confidante, a love who will never outgrow us, leave us, or change her behavior toward us is surely one of the greatest gifts of life.

7. Engage in rituals.

Performing a task or celebration in the same way week after week or year after year gives us a sense of stability, a feeling of being grounded, a sense of security. Even the ritual of pouring a cup of coffee before settling down to work, eating dinner as a family, having lunch at a special restaurant on Fridays, or writing daily in a journal can be significant in dealing with change. Performing rituals and celebrating holidays in a certain way, gives us the satisfaction that not everything is changing.

8. Eliminate the tolerations in your life.

Get rid of the little irritations (and sometimes big ones) that drain your energy, energy you need to manage change. A toleration can be something as simple as a missing button or as significant as a toxic person.

9. **Keep a daily journal.**

When change is viewed over a period of time there is more sense to it. Seeing this historical perspective of past change in our life can give us more objectivity to meet the current changes that are facing us.

10. **Engage in meditation.**

Being centered within yourself grounds you for the changes you're required to face every day. Take a moment to quiet your mind, your body, your soul. You'll reap the rewards of this gift you give yourself.

5. How to Deal With Difficult Employees

If you've been a manager for long, you know that things can go wrong even in the best of organizations. Problem behavior on the part of employees can erupt for a variety of reasons. Here are ten tips for dealing with it.

1. Recognize that problem behavior usually has a history.

It usually develops over time and seldom from a single incident. As a manager, it is your responsibility to be alert to the early warning signs and deal with the underlying causes before the situation reaches a crisis.

2. Ask yourself: "Am I partly or wholly responsible?"

You would be surprised how frequently it is the manager who has created, or at least contributed to problems of employee behavior. Having an abrasive style, being unwilling to listen, and being inattentive to the nuances of employee behavior are all factors that contribute to the manager's need to thoroughly examine what is going on.

3. Don't focus only on the overt behavior.

When confronted by an angry employee, it's easy to attack the person and target the behavior rather than examine the factors that underlie the behavior. Often, this takes patience, careful probing, and a willingness to forgo judgment until you really understand the situation.

4. Be attentive to the "awkward silence" and to what may be missing.

When an employee is obviously reluctant to communicate, it's almost a sure sign that more lurks beneath the surface. Often, employees will withhold because they feel unsafe. They may test the waters by airing a less severe or kindred issue in order to see what kind of a response they get. In order to get the full story and encourage forthrightness, it's imperative that the manager read between the lines and offer the concern and support necessary to get the employee to open up.

5. **Clarify before your confront.**

Chances are, when an issue first surfaces, you will be given only a fragmentary and partial picture of the problem. You may have to dig deep to surface important facts, and talk to others who may be involved. One safe assumption is that each person will tend to present the case from his or her viewpoint, which may or may not be the way it really is. Discretion and careful fact-finding are often required to get a true picture.

6. **Be willing to explore the possibility that you have contributed to the problem.**

This isn't easy, even if you have reason to believe it's so, because you may not be fully aware of what you have done to fuel the fire. Three helpful questions to ask yourself: "Is this problem unique, or does it have a familiar ring as having happened before?", "Are others in my organization exhibiting similar behaviors?", and finally, "Am I partially the cause of the behavior I am criticizing in others?"

7. **Plan your strategy.**

Start by defining, for yourself, what changes you would like to see take place, Then, follow this sequence: (1) Tell the person that there is a problem. State the problem as you understand it and explain why it is important that it be resolved; (2) Gain agreement that you've defined the problem correctly, and that the employee understands that it must be solved; (3) Ask for solutions, using open-ended questions such as: "What are you willing to do to correct this problem?" In some cases, you may have to make it clear what you expect; (4) Get a commitment that the employee will take the required actions; (5) Set deadlines for completing the actions. In the case of a repeated problem, you may want to advise the employee of the consequences of failing to take corrective action; (6) Follow up on the deadlines you've set.

8. Treat the employee as an adult and expect adult behavior.

To some extent, expectation defines the result. If you indicate, by your actions or by the content or tone of your voice, that you expect less than full adult behavior, that's what you're likely to get.

9. Treat interpersonal conflicts differently.

If the problem behavior stems from a personality conflict between two employees, have each one answer these questions: (1) How would you describe the other person?; (2) How does he or she make you feel?; (3) Why do you feel that the other person behaves the way he/she does?; (4) What might you be able to do to alleviate the situation?; (5) What would you like the other person to do in return?.

10. Seek agreement regarding steps to be taken and results expected.

Nothing is really "fixed" unless it stays fixed. All parties to a dispute must agree that the steps taken (or proposed) will substantially alleviate the problem. Further, they must agree on what they will do IF the results attained are not as anticipated. This can be achieved by doing a simple role play, i.e., having each side (including your own) articulate the steps to be taken and the outcomes anticipated. That way, even if subsequent events are significantly different than expected, the lines of communication for adjusting the situation are opened.

6. Effective Business Negotiation Techniques

Learning how to negotiate removes pressure, stress and friction from your life. You see, negotiating is like chess -- if you don't know how to play you will be intimidated by the activity, especially if your opponent knows the game. Negotiating is a predicable event that has rules, planned moves, and counter moves. But, unlike chess, negotiating is an activity you can't avoid, so learn the rules. This article discusses the five underlying facts about negotiating, win-win negotiating, and the definition of a good negotiator.

Five Underlying Facts About Negotiating

1. You are negotiating all the time. Whether you are buying supplies, selling products or services, discussing pay with employees, buying a car, disagreeing with your spouse, or dealing with your children, you are always negotiating. It's just that some of what you negotiate, are considered by you as normal activity.

2. Everything you want is presently owned or controlled by someone else. Doesn't that statement seem like "a given?" But think of the implications. To get what you want means you have to negotiate with the person that has it.

3. There are predictable responses to strategic maneuvers or gambits. It is critical to understand this because if strategies are predictable then they can be managed. If a gambit such as "nibbling" for extras at the end of a negotiation is employed on you then you can request "trade-offs" to either stop it or get extras for yourself.

4. There are three critical factors to every negotiation:

The understanding of power -- Who has the power in the negotiation? Understanding this will help you in your strategies. Does the person you are dealing with have the power to make the decision? Are you in a weak negotiating position? If so, can you bring in factors or strategies that mitigate that?

The information factor -- What the opponent wants, what they require, and understanding the elements about the object negotiated for are all informational items that are critical for a smooth negotiation or to use to your advantage.

The time element -- Time is an important element to negotiation. If someone wants your product but is desperate because they need it quickly, it's a big factor in the strength of your position. You know they have little time to compare other products. You can guarantee speed for more money.

5. People are different and have different personality styles that must be accounted for in negotiations.

Strategies are affected by the people within the negotiation. If you play to the needs and desires of the person, you will be more successful in the negotiation.

Win-Win Negotiating

Understanding the underlying facts about negotiations gives you a base to work from in any negotiation, but win-win is a central theme that must be concentrated on. Keep in mind three simple rules:

1. Never narrow negotiations down to one issue. Doing so leaves the participants in the position of having a winner or a loser. When single-issue negotiations become a factor, broaden the scope of the negotiations. If immediate delivery is important to a customer and you can't meet the schedule, maybe a partial shipment will resolve their problem while you produce the rest.

2. Never assume you know what the other party wants. What you think you are negotiating for may be totally different from what they are. You may be selling them on quality, when what they need is medium quality, low price and large volume. Always keep an eye on their wants and needs.

3. Understand that people are different and have different perspectives on negotiations. Some may want to negotiate and build a long term business relationship. Others may want the deal, and a handshake and it's over. Price is generally an important factor but never assume that money is the only issue. Other issues can change the price they are willing to accept or the price you are willing to accept, like financing, quality, and speed.

The Negotiator

Let's now direct our attention to the negotiator - You. To be a good negotiator requires five things:

1. Understand that negotiating is always a two-way affair - If you ignore that fact, you will ignore the needs of the other party and put a stake in the heart of the negotiation.

2. Desire to acquire the skills of negotiating - Negotiating is a learned activity. Constantly evaluate your performance and determine how you can improve.

3. Understand how the human factor and gambits affect negotiating - Knowing one gambit and using it always is not enough. It may not work on some people. They may have an affective counter to the gambit. Then you are lost or may not recognize tactics being used on you.

4. Be willing to practice - Pay attention to what you are doing during negotiations. Plan them and re-evaluate your performance. Prepare for negotiations by practicing with someone.

5. Desire to create Win-Win situations - You don't want to negotiate with someone who only wants to destroy you. If you both win, a future deal is possible.

As you understand the rules and the process of negotiations, the stress, pressure and friction that currently get in your way will disappear. You will actually learn to enjoy the process.

7. How To Set and Achieve Goals

Life is a journey. Not just any journey, but the most fantastic journey in the universe. Life is a journey from where you are to where you want to be. You can choose your own destination. Not only that, you can choose how you are going to get there. Goal setting will help you end up where you want to be.

-- When it comes to setting goals, start off with what's important to you in life. Take out a sheet of paper. Sit quietly, and on that sheet of paper, brainstorm what you want to accomplish between now and the end of your life.

-- Second step-use another sheet of paper, and this time consider yourself and your personal goals for the next 12 month period. Some key areas in which you might set personal goals include: family, personal growth, financial, health, social, career, hobbies, spiritual, and recreation. Write down the things that you plan to accomplish or achieve or attain during this one-year period?

-- Now, as a third step, go back and compare the two goal lists you have made. Make sure that the items on your short-term list will, as you attain them, be helping you attain your long-term or lifetime goals. It is important that what you are doing short term is taking you in the right direction toward your lifetime goals. Please rewrite your short term goals now if you need to.

-- As a next step, looking at the goals that are on your list at this time, if there are any that you are not willing to pay the price for, go ahead and cross them out, leaving only those items you are willing to cause to happen in your life. This does not necessarily mean you have the money or the other resources for attaining the goal right now. However, when you do have it, would you spend it on or trade it for the goals you have on your list?

-- Now, on still another sheet of paper, create the job goals that are important to you during this upcoming 12-month period. Identify what outcomes you wish to attain or achieve during this one-year period in your specific area of responsibility and authority.

-- Some key areas in which you might consider writing job goals, if you did not already, include: quality, quantity, cost control, cost improvement, equipment, procedures, training, sales, financial, and personnel.

-- As a next step, look for the blending between your job or work goals and your personal goals. Anywhere you notice that you are attaining a goal on the job while at the same time you are attaining a personal goal, note this relationship: it is in these areas you will be most highly motivated.

-- For each of the three lists that you have just created, take an additional sheet of paper and list the activities that you must do to attain the most important goal that you have on each of your lists.

-- Now on another piece of paper titled "Things To-Do List" identify from the activities you just listed, the ones that you must do tomorrow to move you toward your most important goal.

-- Rewrite your goals in these categories at least every three months.

-- The only thing in life that is constant is the fact that everything is changing. It makes sense that our goals will change as we change.

-- Recognize how focusing on what you do want, what you do intend to accomplish, also defines what you choose not to do in your life.

Daily rewrite your list of "Things To-Do" after first reviewing your desired goals.

-- Success is defined as "the progressive realization of a worthwhile goal." If you are doing the things that are moving you toward the attainment of your goal, then you are "successful" even if you are not there yet.

-- Every step along the way to achieving a goal is just as important as the last step.

-- It is not the achieving of a goal that is so important, it is what you become in the process.

-- Set goals with your family also. Help children learn this process early in life.

-- Decide what you should be accomplishing and then stick to your knitting. Do not attempt to be or do all things for all people.

-- Dreams and wishes are not goals until they are written as specific end results on paper.

-- Written specific goals provide direction and focus to your activities. They become a road map to follow.

-- Being busy with activities does not pay, only results do. As in baseball you only get points for getting to the goal of home plate. Just making it to the bases does not count.

-- It has been said that the amount of information available to us is now doubling in less than 30 months. We must learn to focus on only what is truly important to our self and our job.

-- Be sure the goals and activities that you are working for are yours and that you really want and desire to achieve them. The commitment is vital to your success in achieving them.

-- When you have a goal that is exciting to you, the life energy flows through you. You are excited about accomplishing it because it is personally meaningful.

-- Create a time line or matrix chart on which you display your goals visually and the dates when you will have them accomplished.

-- Continually look for ways to integrate or blend personal and professional goals.

-- Setting a goal, that you believe is unattainable will result in frustration. To be challenging and motivating, goals must be perceived as realistic and attainable.

-- Those people with dreams are the ones most likely to experience them.

-- Set goals carefully for you will attain them. This also means if you set none, you will attain that.

-- Goals, when thoughtfully set, can provide strong motivational direction.

-- Clear cut, understandable and realistic objectives leading to the goal help to maintain the sense of realism and the hope of attainment of the goal.

-- Establish measurement criteria to monitor progressive movement toward your goal. Then you will experience progress.

-- Set goals that you will be proud to have achieved, then sense your having completed them.

-- Have a vision that you know is unquestionably right and you will be internally driven to achieve that vision.

-- A goal is "reasonable" when you can see the entire process needed to get to its attainment.

-- Good planning assists in sensing reasonableness of challenging goals.

-- Use picture goals.

-- Develop an emotional reason why you should attain your goal.

8. Effective Delegating Strategies

Delegating work, responsibility, and authority is difficult in a company because it means letting others make decisions which involve spending the owner-manager's money. At a minimum, you should delegate enough authority to get the work done, to allow assistants to take initiative, and to keep the operation moving in your absence.

This Guide discusses controlling those who carry responsibility and authority and coaching them in self-improvement. It emphasizes the importance of allowing competent assistants to perform in their own style rather than insisting that things be done exactly as the owner-manager would personally do them.

"Let others take care of the details."

That, in a few words, is the meaning of delegating work and responsibility.

In theory, the same principles for getting work done through other people apply whether you have 25 employees and one top assistant or 150 to 200 employees and several managers. Yet, putting the principles into practice is often difficult.

Delegation is perhaps the hardest job owner-managers have to learn. Some never do. They insist on handling many details and work themselves into early graves. Others pay lip service to the idea but actually run a one-man shop. They give their assistants many responsibilities but little or no authority.

How Much Authority?

Authority is the fuel that makes the machine go when you delegate work and responsibility. It poses a question: To what extent do you allow another person to make decisions which involve spending your company's money?

That question is not easy to answer. Sometimes, an owner-manager has to work it out as he goes along, as did Tom Brasser. His pride in being the top man made it hard for him to share authority. He tried, but he found to his dismay that his delegating was not as good as he thought.

One day when he returned from his first short business trip. Mr. Brasser stormed out of his office. He waved a sheaf of payroll sheets and shouted "Who approved all this overtime while I was away?" I did," the production chief answered.

Realizing that all heads were turned to see what the shouting was about., Mr. Brasser lowered his voice. Taking the production manager with him, he stepped into his office.

There he told the production man, "You've got your nerve authorizing overtime. This is still my company, and I'll decide what extra costs we'll take on. You know good and well that our prices are not based on paying overtime rates."

"Right," the production man replied. "But you told me I was in full charge of production. You said I should keep pushing so I wouldn't fall behind on deliveries."

"That's right," Mr. Brasser said. "In fact, I recall writing you about a couple of orders just before I went out of town."

"You can say that again. And one of them - the big order - was getting behind so I approved overtime."

"I would have done the same thing if I has been here," Mr. Brasser said. "But let's get things straight for the future. From now on, overtime needs my okay. We've got to keep costs in line."

Mr. Brasser then followed up with his other department heads, including his office manager and purchasing agent. He called them in, told them what had happened, and made it clear that their authority did not include making decisions that would increase the company's operating costs. Such decisions had to have his approval, he pointed out, because it was his company. He was the one who would lose, if and when, increased costs ate up the profit.

Yet, if an owner-manager is to run a successful company, you must delegate authority properly. How much authority is proper depends on your situation.

At a minimum, you should delegate enough authority:

(1) To get the work done,

(2) To allow key employees to take initiative, and

(3) To keep things going in your absence.

To Whom Do You Delegate?

Delegation of responsibility does not mean that you say to your assistants, "Here, you run the shop." The people to whom you delegate responsibility and authority must be competent in the technical areas for which you hold them accountable. However, technical competence is not enough.

In addition, the person who fills a key management spot in the organization must either be a manager or be capable of becoming one. A manager's chief job is to plan, direct, and coordinate the work of others.

A manager should possess the three "I's" - initiative, interest, and imagination. The manager of a department must have enough self-drive to start and keep things moving. A manager should not have to be told, for example, to make sure that employees start work on time.

Personality traits must be considered. A key manager should be strong- willed enough to overcome opposition when necessary and should also have enough ego to want to "look good" but not so much that it antagonizes other employees.

Spell Out the Delegation

Competent people want to know for what they are being held responsible. The experience of Charles P. Wiley illustrates how one owner-manager let them know. He started by setting up an organization. He broke his small company into three departments: a production department, a sales department, and an administrative department.

The manager who handled production was responsible for advertising, customer solicitations, and customer service. Mr. Wiley regarded the administrative department as the headquarters and service unit for the other two. Its manager was responsible for personnel, purchasing, and accounting.

Mr. Wiley also worked out with his assistants the practices and procedures necessary to get the jobs done. His assistants were especially helpful in pointing out any overlaps or gaps in assigned responsibilities. He then put the procedures into writing. Thus each supervisor had a detailed statement of the function of each's department and the extent of each's authority.

This statement included a list of specific actions which they could take on their own initiative and a list of actions which required approval in the front office - Mr. Wiley, or in his absence, the assistant general manager.

Mr. Wiley had thought about the times when he might be absent from the plant. To make sure that things would keep moving, the production manager was designated assistant general manager and given authority to make all operational decisions in Mr. Wiley's absence.

In thinking about absences, Mr. Wiley went one step further. He instructed each department head to designate and train an assistant who could run the department if, and when, the need arose.

When you spell out the delegation, be sure that departments are coordinated. The experience of another small plant owner, Ann Jones, is a case in point. She thought her departments were coordinated until the shop manager reported that he was swamped with "rush" orders.

"It's impossible for me to make good on Bill's promise," the shop chief said. Bill was the sales manager.

When Bill was called in, he said "I had to promise early delivery to get the business."

Ms. Jones resolved the problem by instructing the sales manager and the shop manager to work out delivery dates together.

Make sure that departments are coordinated when you spell out the responsibilities and authority of each key manager. Thus you reduce the
chances of confusion as well as assuring that there is no doubt about who is responsible for specific jobs. Then, the particular key manager can take corrective action before things get out of hand.

Keeping Control

When you manage through others, it is essential that you keep control. You do it by holding a subordinate responsible for his or her actions and checking the results of those actions.

In controlling your assistants, try to strike a balance. You should not get into a key manager's operation so closely that you stifle him or her should you be so far removed that you lose control of things.

You need feedback to keep yourself informed. Reports provide a way to get the right kind of feedback at the right time. They can be daily, weekly, or monthly, depending on how soon you need the information. Each department head can report his or her progress, or the lack of it, in the unit of production that is appropriate for his or her activity; for example, items packed in the shipping room, sales per territory, hours of work per employee.

Periodic staff meetings are another way to get feedback. At these meetings, department heads can comment on their activities, accomplishments, and problems.

Coaching Your Staff

For the owner-manager, delegation does not end with good control. It involves coaching as well, because management ability is not acquired automatically. You have to teach it.

Just as important, you have to keep your managers informed just as you would be if you were doing their jobs. Part of your job is to see that they get the facts they need for making their decisions.

You should be certain that you convey your thinking when you coach your assistants. Sometimes words can be inconsistent with your thoughts. Ask questions to make sure the listener understands your meanings. In other words, delegation can only be effective when you have good communications.

And above all, listen. Many owner-managers get so involved in what they are saying or are going to say next, that they do not listen to the other person. In coaching a person so he or she can improve, it is important to tell why you give the instruction. When a person knows the reason, he or she is better able to supervise.

Allow Staff to Work

Sometimes you find yourself involved in many operational details even though you do everything that is necessary for delegating responsibility. In spite of defining authority, delegating to competent persons, spelling out the delegation, keeping control, and coaching, you are still burdened with detailed work. Why? Usually, you have failed to do one vital things. You have refused to stand back and let the wheels turn.

If you are to make delegation work, you must allow your managers freedom to do things their way. You and the company are in trouble if you try to measure your assistants by whether or not they do a particular task exactly as you would do it. They should be judged by their results - not their methods.

No two persons react exactly the same in every situation. Be prepared to see some action taken differently from the way in which you would do it even though your policies are well defined. Of course, if an assistant strays too far from policy, you need to bring him or her back into line. You cannot afford second-guessing.

You should also keep in mind that when an owner-manager second-guesses assistants, you risk destroying their self-confidence. If the assistant does not run his or her department to your satisfaction and if his or her department to your satisfaction and if his or her shortcomings cannot be overcome, then replace that person. But when results prove his or her effectiveness, it is good practice to avoid picking at each move he or she makes.

9. How To Ensure the Profitability of Your Business

Why do some business owner-managers hit the profit target more often than others? They do it because they keep their operation pointed in that direction - direction of profit making. They never lose sight of the goal - to finish the year with a profit.

This guide gives suggestions that should help an owner-manager to zero in on profit making. It points out that you must keep informed, make timely decisions, and take effective action. In effect you must control the activities of your company rather than being controlled by them.

A beginner rarely shoots a hole in one, hits a bull's-eye, or hooks a prize winning trout. Topnotch performance in golf, shooting, and fishing requires knowledge, practice, and perseverance.

Similarly, in small businesses, year-end profit comes to the owner-manager who strives for topnotch performance. You achieve profit making goals by knowing your operation, by practicing the art of making timely, balanced judgments and by controlling the company's activities.

Adapt the suggestions in this guide to your situation. They should help you call the shots to keep your company headed in the right direction - toward profit making.

First Rule of Profit Making: Know Your Business

The time-honored truth "Knowledge is power" is especially pertinent to the owner-manager of a small business. To keep your company pointed toward profit you must keep yourself well informed about it. You must know how the company is doing before you can improve its operation. You must know its weak points before you can correct them. Some of the knowledge you need you pick up from day-to-day personal observation, but records should be your principal source of information about profits, costs, and sales.

Know Your Profit. The profit and loss statement (or income statement) prepared regularly each month or each quarter by your accountant is one of the most vital indicators of your business's worth and health. You should make sure that this statement contains all the facts you need for evaluating your profit. This statement must pinpoint each revenue and cost area. For example, it should show the profit and loss for each of your products and product lines as well as the profit and loss for your entire operation.

It is a good idea to have your profit and loss statement prepared so that it shows each item for the current period, for the same period last year, and for the current year-to-date. For example, a P&L statement for the month of November would show income and expenses for the current month, for November last year, and totals for the eleven months of the current year. Many corporations publish their annual reports with several previous years so stockholders can compare earnings.

Comparison is the key to using your P&L statement. If your accountant is not already furnishing figures that you can compare, you should discuss the possibility of having them provided.

Financial ratios from your balance sheet also help you to know if your profit is what it should be. For example, the ratio of net worth (return on investment ratio) shows what the business earned on the equity capital invested.

Know Your Costs. An owner-manager should know costs in detail. Then, you can compare your cost figures as a percentage of sales (operating ratio). Be certain that your costs are itemized so that you can put your fingers on those that seem to be rising or falling according to your experience and the cost figures of your industry. When costs are itemized, you can spot the culprit when the overall figure is higher than what you had budgeted. Take advertising costs for example. You can catch the offender if you break out your advertising expenditures by product lines and by media. In addition, a thorough check of inquiry returns from advertising will help to avoid unproductive publications.

In knowing your costs, keep in mind that the formula for profit is: Profit equals Sales minus Costs.

Know Your Product Markup. Be certain that the pricing of your products provides a markup adequate for the kind of profit you expect to achieve. You must keep constantly informed on pricing because you have to adjust for rising costs and at the same time keep prices competitive. Knowledge about your markup also helps you to run close outs with your eyes open. Continuing to make a product that only a few customers want is an effective merchandising tool only when you use it on purpose - for example, to hold or attract buyers for other high markup products. Don't hesitate to drop a loser from your line.

Garbage-In, Garbage-Out. An owner-manager should not fudge the records. The acronym GIGO that the computer industry uses is true with manually kept records as well as with machine-processed ones. If an owner-manager allows "garbage" to go into the records, the reports will contain "garbage." Reports need not be extensive but they must be accurate.

Look For Trends. Try not to look at a single month's sales or profit picture by itself. The figures on your operating statements are meaningful only when you put the picture in the right frame - that is, look at your figures in the context of what has happened and what is likely to happen. In that manner, you catch a downward trend before it gets out of hand.

You should also concern yourself with the figures behind the dollars - for example, the number of units sold or the number of orders. Insist on cost-per-unit statistics. The fluctuation of the cost-per-unit can be much more meaningful than just looking at the dollar figures alone. Another idea is to display these comparative figures on graphs so that significant trends can be seen easily.

Predict Your Future

Don't use a crystal ball to make forecasts of your business. By carefully analyzing the historic trends of your business, as shown in your records for the past five years, you can forecast for the year ahead. Your record of sales, your experience with the markets in which you sell, and your general knowledge of the economy should enable you to forecast a sales figure for the next year.

When you have a sales forecast figure, make up a budget showing your costs as a percentage of that figure. In the next year, you can compare actual P&L figures to your budgeted figures. Thus, your budget is an important tool for determining the health of your business.

Make Timely Decisions

Without action, forecasts and decisions about the future are not worth the paper they are written on. A decision that does not result in action is a poor one. The pace of business demands timely as well as informed decision making. If the owner-manager is to stay ahead of competition, you must move to control your destiny.

Effective decision making in the small business requires several things. The owner-manager must have as much accurate information as possible. With these facts, you should determine the consequences of all feasible courses of action and the time requirements. When you have made the judgment, you have set up your business so that the decisions you make can be transmitted into action.

Control Your Business

To be effective, the owner-manager must be able to motivate key people to get the results planned for within the cost and time limits allowed. In working to achieve results, the small business owner-manager has an advantage over big business. You can be fast and flexible while many large firms must await committee action before a decision is made. You do not have to get permission to act. And equally important, bottlenecks to implementing new practices can receive your personal attention.

One of the secrets is in deciding what items to control. Even in a small company, the owner-manager should not try to be all things to everyone. You should keep close control on people, products, money, and any other resources that you consider significant to keeping your operation pointed toward profit.

Manage Your People. Most businesses find that their largest expense is labor. Yet because of the close contact with employees, some owner-manager of small businesses do not pay enough attention to direct and indirect labor costs. They tend to think of these costs in terms of individuals rather than relate them to profit in terms of dollars and cents.

Here are a few suggestions concerning personnel management:

1. Periodically review each position in your company. Take a quarterly look at the job. Is work being duplicated? Is it structured so that it encourages the employee to become involved? Can the tasks be given to another employee or employees and a position eliminated? Can a part-time person fill the job.

2. Play a little private mental game. Imagine that you must get rid of one employee, If you had to let one person go, who would it be? How would you realign the jobs to make out? You may find a real solution to the imaginary problem is possible to your financial benefit.

3. Use compensation as a tool rather than viewing it as a necessary evil. Reward quality work. Investigate the possibility of using raises and bonuses as incentives for higher productivity. For example, can you schedule bonuses as morale boosters during seasonal slacks or other dull periods?

4. Remember that there are new ways of controlling absenteeism through incentive compensation plans.

For example, the owner-manager of one small company eliminated vacations and sick leave. Instead, this owner-manager gave each employee thirty days annual leave to use as the employee saw fit. At the end of the year, the employees were paid at regular rates for the leave they didn't use. To qualify for the year-end pay, the employee had to prove that sick leave was taken only for that purpose. Non-sick leave had to be applied for in advance. As a result, unscheduled absences and overtime pay were reduced significantly. In addition, employees were happier and more productive than they were under the old system.

Control Your Inventory. Don't tie up all your money in inventory. Use a perpetual inventory system as a cost control rather than a system just for tax purposes. Establish use patterns or purchase patterns on the materials or items you must stock to keep the minimum number required to supply your customers or to maintain production. Excessive inventory, whether it is finished product or raw materials, ties up funds that could be used to better advantage, for example, to open up a new sales territory or to buy new machinery.

Centralize your purchases and avoid duplications. Be a comparative shopper. Confirm orders in writing. Get the price and amount straight right away.

Check what you receive for condition and quality. Check bills from suppliers against quotations. You do not want to be the victim of their error.

You should, however, keep one fact in mind when you set up your inventory control system. Do not spend more on the control system than it will return in savings.

Control Your Products. From control of inventory to control of products is but a step. Make sure that your sales people recognize the importance of selling the products that are the most profitable. Align your service policies with your markup in mind. Arrange your goods so that low markup items require the least handling.

Control Your Money. It is good policy to handle cash and checks as though they were perishable commodities. They are. Money in your safe earns no return; and it can be stolen. Bank promptly.

Use credit wisely and take advantage of discounts. One of the hallmarks of a successful business owner-manager is knowing how much credit you can afford to extend over any period and how much you have already extended. Grant credit willingly, but keep it on a systematic basis. Insist on a written credit application and see that the credit application contains a promise to pay according to the credit practice in your industry.

Get your monthly bills out to customers on time, and be certain that bills show date of purchases, what was purchased, how much it cost, and how much was paid, if anything, and then how much is owned. The statement should also show your customer any overdue balance and for how long it has been overdue.

Every account will not pay promptly but keep in mind that a slow paying customer can be profitable, especially if the customer buys large amounts of your high markup items. The danger is in letting such a customer get in beyond the ability to pay. Set up a system for collecting from late and slow paying accounts, but in reminding them to pay up, your objective is to get your money without losing their business.

Get Help When You Need It

It is good practice to use your outside advisors as you go along rather than calling on them only in emergencies. For example, your accountant can help you analyze the financial position of your business to help you avoid problems rather than to get you out of them.

Sometimes an owner-manager needs to call in a management consultant. For example, help may be needed in isolating and solving a problem that the owner-manager senses but can't quite put a finger on. In other instances, the consultant's professional background may be needed to supply skills that do not exist in the company - for example, the capability for doing market research or for setting up an inventory control system. In many cases, the management consultant can provide the time that the owner/manager lacks to implement a solution.

10. How to Create a Business Environment that Supports Growth

Manage a business effectively, manage staff effectively, is the key to the establishment and growth of the business. The key to successful management is to examine the marketplace environment and create employment and profit opportunities that provide the potential growth and financial viability of the business. Despite the importance of management, this area is often misunderstood and poorly implemented, primarily because people focus on the output rather than the process of management.

Toward the end of the 1980s, business managers became absorbed in improving product quality, sometimes ignoring their role vis-a-vis personnel. The focus was on reducing costs and increasing output, while ignoring the long-term benefits of motivating personnel. This shortsighted view tended to increase profits in the short term, but created a dysfunctional long-term business environment.

Simultaneously with the increase in concern about quality, entrepreneurship attracted the attention of business. A sudden wave of successful entrepreneurs seemed to render earlier management concepts obsolete. The popular press focused on the new cult heroes Steve Jobs and Steve Wozniack (creators and developers of the Apple Computer) while ignoring the marketing and organizing talents of Mike Markula, the executive responsible for Apple's business plan. The story of two guys selling their Volkswagen bus to build the first Apple computer was more romantic than that of the organizational genius that enabled Apple to develop, market and ship its products while rapidly becoming a major corporation.

In large businesses, effective manage business skills requires planning. Planning is essential for developing a firm's potential. However, many small businesses do not recognize the need for long-range plans, because the small number of people involved in operating the business implies equal responsibility in the planning and decision-making processes. Nevertheless, the need for planning is as important in a small business as it is in a large one.

This guide focuses on the importance of good management practices. Specifically, it addresses the responsibilities of managing the external and internal environments.

MANAGING THE EXTERNAL ENVIRONMENT

Three decades ago, Alvin Toffler suggested that the vision of the citizen in the tight grip of an omnipotent bureaucracy would be replaced by an organizational structure of ad-hocracy. The traditional business organization implied a social contract between employees and employers. By adhering to a fixed set of obligations and sharply defined roles and responsibilities, employees received a predefined set of rewards.

The organizational structure that Toffler predicted in 1970 became the norm 20 years later, and with it came changed concepts of authority. As organizations became more transitory, the authority of the organization and firm was replaced by the authority of the individual manager. This entrepreneurial management model is now being replicated throughout society. As a result, the individual business owner must internalize ever increasing organizational functions.

Another change in today's business environment is dealing with government agencies. Their effect on the conduct of business most recently appears to have increased. As industries fail to achieve high levels of ethical behavior or individual businesses exhibit specific lapses, the government rushes in to fill the breach with its regulations.

MANAGING THE INTERNAL ENVIRONMENT

HUMAN RESOURCE ISSUES

Ensuring Open Communications

Effective communications play an integral role in managing and operating any successful business. With open communications changes and their effects on the organization are quickly shared. Your firm then has the time and skills needed to respond to changes and take advantage of evolving opportunities.

The following checklist addressing how you would respond to an employee's suggestion provides an assessment of the communication process in your business. Place a check next to the statements that are commonly heard in your business.

Statement

Face facts it's unrealistic. -----

Who else has done it? -----

It's not your problem. -----

Fill out form XX/xx revised. -----

It won't work. -----

Bring it to the committee. -----

We don't have the time. -----

We tried it before and it failed. -----

You think what? You're joking! -----

Everybody knows that that's foolish. -----

We can't afford to think about it. -----

Don't you have better things to do? -----

Are you some kind of a radical? -----

We're too small/big for that. -----

Impossible; our main product line would be obsolete. -----

The boss would never consider it. -----

It's contrary to company policy. -----

Carefully consider any statements that you have checked. This may indicate that management is inflexible and unresponsive to employee suggestions. Management that is unable to respond immediately to changes in the market signals an inflexible unstable firm. In the rapidly changing business environment such management can mean eventual failure for your business. If you haven't developed such a checklist do so. It will help you determine if and where adjustments are needed in your management staff.

Balancing Schedules Stress and Personnel

Without organization and good management the compressed time schedules associated with modern business can cause stress and make extraordinary demands on people. An effective management structure can reduce stress and channel the productive capacity of employees into business growth and profits.

Setting Duties Tasks and Responsibilities

An organization is characterized by the nature and determination of employees' duties tasks and responsibilities. While many organizations use different methods for determining these it is essential that they be clearly defined.

The core of any organization is its people and their functions. Duties tasks and responsibilities often evolve in an ad hoc manner. A typical firm starts with a few people often one performing all duties. As the firm grows others are hired to fill specific roles often on a functional basis. Roles that were handled by consultants and specialists outside the firm now are handled internally. As new needs emerge new roles are developed.

Just as an emerging business develops an accounting system it should also develop a human resource system. For instance the following employee information should be available and checked for accuracy at least once each year.

- Name

- Address

- Nationality (immigration status)

- Marital status and dependents

- Hire date

- Company job history:

- Title and code

- Performance

- Location

- Salary rate and history

- Education including degrees

- Specialty training

- Transcripts as appropriate

- Pre-employment work experience:

- Key responsibilities and levels

- Professional licenses or certificates

- Professional publication and speaking engagements

- Teaching experience

- Language abilities:

- Reading

- Writing

- Speaking

- Leadership evidence:

- Company

- Civic

- Other

- Relocation preferences and limitations

- Travel experience and preferences

- Career goals

Review your personnel files periodically to ensure that the information is correct and current. Implement a system that will make updating personnel files a fairly simple routine yet confidential process.

Business Team

The apex of an effective organization lies in developing the business team. Such a team involves delegating authority and increasing productivity. Assess the effectiveness of your business team with the following checklist:

The leader of the team is respected by the members. -----

The abilities of all team members are respected. -----

A team spirit is evident through activities. -----

Individual members compensate for weaknesses in each other. -----

Jokes are not disparaging. -----

A genuine feeling of being part of the best is exuded. -----

The work area is self-delineated and reflects a spirit. -----

Mistakes result in corrective action not retribution. -----

Each member understands the importance of his or her contribution. -----

The team can explore new areas of activity. -----

Security of employment is evident. -----

Controlling Conflict

Another key to successful management lies in controlling conflict. Conflict cannot be eliminated from either the business or the interpersonal activities of the enterprise. A measure of the organization's success is the degree to which conflict can be exposed and the energies associated with it channeled to develop the firm. Although establishing policies and procedures represents the tangible aspect of organization and management the mechanisms to tolerate and embody challenges to the established operation serve as the real essence of a firm that will survive and prosper.

Structural Issues

Organization

The effectiveness of a particular organizational form depends on a variety of internal and external events for example:

Competitors (number or activity)

Technology (internal or external)

Regulatory environment

Customer characteristics

Supplier characteristics

Economic environment

Key employees

Growth

Strategy (including new products and markets)

Even though you may discover that certain events are affecting your business be careful not to change the organizational structure of your firm without discussing it with your management team. Employees generally can accomplish goals despite organizational structures imposed by management. Because restructuring involves spending a lot of time learning new rules implementing a new organizational structure is costly.

Structure

The essence of a successful organization can be more simply summarized than implemented. The following checklist can help you determine measures to ensure your management structure is adequate. Check the entries that apply to your firm and also find out what measures your company needs to take to improve its management structure.

Key market and customers are understood. -----

Technology is mastered. -----

Key objectives are articulated and shared. -----

Major functions are identified and staffed. -----

A hierarchy of relationships is established. -----

A business team is in place and functioning. -----

Measurable results are well above industry standards. -----

Employees are the best source of new hires. -----

Policy and Procedural Issues

Authority

The central element of organizational management is authority. Through authority your firm develops the structure necessary to achieve its objectives.

A. L. Stinchcombe summarized the role of authority succinctly when he stated any administrative system that decides on the use of resources is also a system of authority directing the activities of people.

The authority that once was conferred by either owning a small business or having a position in the bureaucracy of a larger firm has been replaced by technical competence (including that of forming and running the business). Forces external to your business may emphasize the elements of granted versus earned authority. Once the owner-manager controlled the entire business but suppliers customers unions and the government have severely limited the ability of the business owner-manager to take independent action.

A primary component of authority is the exercise of control within the organization. A thorough system of controls ensures the firm's operation and provides a mechanism for imposing authority. Internal controls include the provision that authority be delegated and circumscribed; examples of these provisions follow. Place a check by the provisions that apply to your firm. Consider implementing controls over areas that you have not checked.

Approval for disbursements of cash and regular accounting. -----

Reconciliation of bank statements. -----

Periodic count and reconciliation of inventory records. -----

Approval of pricing policies and exemptions. -----

Approval of credit policies and exemptions. -----

Review of expense and commission accounts. -----

Approval of purchasing and receiving policies. -----

Review of payments to vendors and employees. -----

Approval of signature authorities for payments. -----

Review of policies. -----

Delegation is a key to the effective exercise of authority in your business. By delegating limited authority to accomplish specific tasks the talents of employees in the organization can be used to upgrade the skills and experience of the manager. The following checklist enables you to determine if you are taking advantage of opportunities to delegate authority.

Is your time consumed by daily chores? -----

Do you have time for the following:

- Training and development of subordinates? -----

- Planning? -----

- Coordinating and controlling work of subordinates? -----

- Visiting customers and subordinates regularly? -----

- Remaining involved in new product development? -----

- Visiting branch locations regularly? -----

- Attending business meetings outside your business? -----

- Participating in civic affairs? -----

Is no one on your staff as good as you are? -----

To effectively delegate responsibility and authority in your organization you must:

Accept the power of delegation.

Know the capabilities of subordinates.

Ensure that specific training is available.

Select specific responsibilities to be delegated.

Clearly define the extent and limits of delegation.

Match each with necessary authority.

Provide periodic monitoring and interest.

Restrain the impulse to insist on how to do something.

Remember there are many ways to accomplish a specific objective.

Assess results and provide appropriate feedback.

Praise and criticize.

The skills and abilities of each level of authority can be increased by effectively delegating authority throughout any organization.

Operating Reports

Operating reports form the organizational basis of your business. Such reports mirror the organization its structure and function. They define key relationships between employees and can either minimize or increase organizational stress.

For many businesses the following reports form the basis for analyzing the specific areas of a business (the frequency of each report depends on the nature size and organization of your business). Check the reports your firm currently generates.

Consider creating reporting systems where they are lacking.

Case reports (daily, weekly, monthly) -----

New orders and backlog (weekly, monthly) -----

Shipments/sales (weekly, monthly) -----

Employment (monthly) -----

Inventory out of stock (weekly, monthly) -----

Product quality (weekly, monthly) -----

Accounts receivable aging accounts (monthly) -----

Weekly overdue accounts -----

Returns and allowances (monthly) -----

Production (weekly, monthly) -----

Reporting must be kept current to allow for timely identification and correction of problems before serious damage to the organization occurs.

Too much reporting as well as inappropriate reporting can be as destructive as too little reporting. For instance the CEO of a major industrial firm who receives daily production and inventory reports by model can lose his or her ability to maintain an overall perspective. Thus operating managers must attempt to identify and solve local problems and take advantage of local opportunities within their own authority. Inappropriate reporting compromises management's ability to leverage individual skills and abilities.

Operating reports not only provide essential data that enable management to accomplish its objectives they also focus staff's attention on the organization's goals. If reporting is not taken seriously employees may deal with customers suppliers and each other in a similarly trivial manner.

To avoid inappropriate reporting review reporting policies annually to ensure that reports are appropriate and contain the information needed to make sound management decisions.

Conclusion

Successful management is founded on the mastery of a myriad of details. While management schools teach the importance of focusing attention on major issues affecting the business practical managers realize the major issues are the variety of small aspects that form the business. In an increasingly structured society inattention to even one minor detail can result in significant disruption of the business or even its failure.

Checklist For An Effective Organization

The following checklist will help you identify and determine the effectiveness of the management and organizational structure of the firm. If you answer yes to most of the following questions you are effectively managing your firm. A no answer indicates that you need to focus on this management issue.

yes / no

Are responsibilities clear and matched by authority? -----

Is your business structure clear yet flexible? -----

Are communications focused on finding solutions rather than placing blame? -----

Do people have the information and resources necessary to do an excellent job? -----

Do you and your employees care about the business? -----

Does staff come in early and stay late on their own initiative? -----

Are mechanisms for conflict resolution working? -----

Is disorder minimized and channeled? -----

Can people joke with and about each other and you? -----

Does a corporate plan spell out the firm's vision? -----

Do employees pitch in unasked during a crisis? -----

Do customers and suppliers prefer to do business with you?

11. How to Conduct Successful Meetings

Was your last meeting successful? Were you an effective chairman or an active participant? Were those who had a contribution to make invited? Did the meeting accomplish the stated purpose? These questions and many more need to be asked and answered affirmatively if organizational meetings are to be successful. The chairman - the one who plans, hosts, and leads a meeting - must establish a proper environment. The environment, and the feeling conveyed to the participants by the chairman, will have a great impact on the outcome of the meeting. The chairman must stimulate, guide, clarify, control, summarize, and evaluate the discussion, keeping in mind his responsibility to accomplish the meeting objectives. If he fails to perform his role effectively, the meeting may turn into meaningless discussions of irrelevant subjects, a series of pointless power plays, and even boring monologues.

Meetings are essential and can serve as an effective method of communication within an organization. They have been rightfully categorized by some managers as time-consuming, high-priced, and un-productive, but this need not be the case. Sometimes we expect too much from a meeting. When it fails to meet our expectations, we may be too quick to criticize. William F. Utterback, author of Group Thinking and Conference Leadership, said, "It must not be supposed that the conference table possesses the magic property of generating wisdom when rubbed simultaneously by a dozen pairs of elbows." Meetings are helpful means of achieving coordination. When there is a gathering of people with a mutual interest, the results may be as follows:

- Encourage participation in the subject of concern;
- Integrate interests;
- Broaden perspectives and change attitudes;
- Improve decision-making; and
- Motivate and commit participants to courses of action.

The fundamental decision concerning meetings is not whether to hold them, but how to make them effective. Recent studies show that members of middle management spend 30 percent of their time in meetings. Unproductive meetings can result in substantial loss to an organization.

On the other hand, a productive meeting becomes a tool for effective management communication, and serves as a vehicle for development of specific plans or the organization of specific tasks. In any case, successful meetings don't just happen; they occur as a result of careful planning, good leadership, and close attention to details before, during, and after the session.

The Planning Process

The key steps to be taken by the chairman in planning a meeting are as follows:

- Establish the meeting objectives;
- Prepare the meeting agenda;
- Determine timing and physical arrangements;
- Identify and invite participants; and

- Consider matters of protocol.

Let's review each of these steps in detail.

Meeting Objectives

Why is the meeting being held? What will it accomplish? Meetings are usually held for one or more of the following reasons:

- To disseminate new information or provide feedback;
- To receive a report;
- To coordinate efforts of a specific nature and obtain group support;
- To win acceptance for a new idea, plan, or system;
- To reconcile a conflict;
- To negotiate an agreement;
- To motivate members of a group;
- To initiate creative thinking within a group; and
- To solve a current problem within a group.

The meeting plan should not be too broad or the meeting may be doomed from the beginning.

Therefore, a wise chairman identifies realistic objectives for the meeting and is prepared to meet them.

Meeting Agenda

Is an agenda necessary? How long will it require to carry out the agenda? Would the meeting run smoothly and be just as successful without it?

The agenda should crystallize the intended meeting objective(s) and establish the time available to accomplish them. Whether the agenda is in writing or stated verbally by the chairman, it provides the framework to keep the meeting on target. Furthermore, it permits the chairman to devote his attention to managing the interplay of the participants.

The meeting should focus on the objective(s) and also on reaching the objective(s) in a pre-established, finite time schedule. Meetings that exceed established time limits usually are not constructive because opinions begin to replace facts. Such meetings are apt to go astray and may even disintegrate into personal contests or power plays between participants. There are several other points to consider during preparation of the agenda. Notable among them are:

Focus the agenda on items relating to the same general topic, if possible. Begin with a discussion of topics of major concern to participants; then, if necessary, discuss related topics of lesser importance. A meeting of this type requires fewer attendees and generates better participation in the discussion.

-Schedule fewer agenda items when the topics cannot be related. It is difficult for most participants to come to a meeting completely prepared on a wide variety of topics. The more concise the agenda, the better.

Attach background data for each topic to be discussed, when the agenda is distributed. This will ensure that each participant has some familiarity with the items before arriving at the meeting.

Establish a time limit and priority for each agenda item. Consider whether the topic to be discussed is familiar, new, controversial, or complex.

Don't have the meeting run too long. One hour is usually the norm for busy middle- to upper-level managers. When the meeting is scheduled on a quarterly, semiannual, or annual basis, it may run longer to accomplish the objectives. Schedule a "break" when the meeting is expected to take over 2 hours.

Submit the agenda to the participants, with the background data, as early as possible. This will give each participant more time to prepare for the meeting.

The chairman should be sure the meeting is needed. If the need disappears, he should cancel the meeting.

Time/Physical Arrangements

When should the meeting be held? Where should it be held? There are several necessary considerations regarding time and physical arrangements for the meeting. Among the more important are:

- The convenience of the place.
- The size of the room. It should not be too large or too small. If the right-size room is not available, it is better to select a small room, rather than too large a room. A small room presents a friendlier atmosphere than a large, sparsely filled one.
- The seating arrangement and the availability of extra seats if needed.
- The lighting, heating, and ventilation.

- Any visual aids required and their proper use.
- Availability of extra paper and pencils.
- The need for name plates or name tags.
- The handling of messages.

It is the chairman's responsibility to begin and end the meeting on time. It is the responsibility of attendees to arrive on time. Two techniques proved effective in curing cases of chronic tardiness are (1) to ignore latecomers; and (2) to make no attempt to bring late-comers up to date.

Meeting Size

How many persons should be invited to the meeting? What is the purpose of inviting each person? The attendees should be viewed as management resources - each able to contribute to the meeting through knowledge or experience or both. It is wise to include some of the persons in the organization to whom action items may be given after the meeting. This tends to encourage better support for the topics to be discussed. Attendance by disinterested persons tends to increase non-relevant discussion and impede the meeting. Thus, the chairman should invite as many people as necessary, but no more.

The size of the meeting tends to affect the way it functions. For example, if attendance exceeds seven, there is a tendency for communication to become more centralized, and participants have less opportunity to communicate directly with one another. As the number of people invited increases, the ability of the chairman to predict the interaction that will take place becomes more difficult.

It is important to have all relevant points of view on a particular subject under consideration represented at the meeting, even if this makes it a large meeting. A large meeting requires increased formality and extra time for each topic to ensure adequate communication between participants.

Proponents of the "small group" theory consider seven to be the maximum number of participants for a productive meeting. However, if a problem-solving type of meeting is to be held, some authorities claim that up to 12 participants can be accommodated effectively. If the number of participants exceeds 18, the chairman may find it almost impossible to accomplish the meeting objectives.

On the other hand, in a meeting involving only three participants, there may be a tendency for two of them to form a combination against the third participant. This could be disastrous so managers should guard against organizing too small a meeting.

Matters Of Protocol

Why should the chairman be concerned about protocol? How can this affect the success of a meeting? One of the initial steps to ensure a successful meeting is to give adequate consideration to protocol. Protocol might be defined as the application of common-sense courtesy.

Some steps the chairman might take to avoid protocol problems are:

- Notify participants well in advance of the meeting date, and provide them with an agenda and background data.
- Notify department heads when subordinates with expertise are needed.
- Make sure that arrangements with resource persons outside the organization are completed before the meeting.
- Introduce resource persons and newcomers at the start of the meeting. Also, make their affiliations and expertise known to the other attendees.
- List participants in alphabetical order in the meeting announcement and minutes, unless someone present far outranks the others. In that case, list this person first.
- Express gratitude to those from outside the group as well as to those within the group for significant contributions to the success of the meeting.
- Advise those invited to attend the meeting of postponement or cancellation as far in advance as possible.

Running the Meeting

The chairman should make the meeting as relaxed and informal as possible. He should resort to Robert's Rules of Order only when attendance is large or debate becomes heated. The chairman should "manage" the meeting, speak when appropriate, encourage discussion, seek a consensus, and summarize. Under no circumstances should the chairman be unprepared, "hog" the discussion, play the comic, chastise a participant, or let the meeting run by itself.

The meeting will not get off the ground unless the participants know where they are going. Therefore, it is important that the chairman make a concerted effort to ensure that:

- Every participant has a clear understanding of the meeting objectives at the start of the meeting.
- Each agenda item has a time allocation. The time limit for the meeting should be announced when the agenda is published, or at the beginning of the meeting.
- The objective(s) remain valid throughout the meeting. If not, they should be revised.

Meeting objective(s) can be communicated more readily if the chairman does not try to force them on the participants. A consensus about the objectives at the beginning will vastly improve chances for success of the meeting.

Do you play your role well at a meeting? For a meeting to succeed, the chairman must display strong leadership and he and the participants must be willing and determined to:

- Become acquainted with each of the participants and carry on a light conversation with them during the "warm-up" session at the beginning of the meeting.
- Give the other participants an opportunity to present their ideas, opinions, and recommendations without interrupting or degrading their comments.
- Listen wisely and well to the other participants.
- Accept new or fresh thoughts and ideas expressed by other participants, provided these thoughts and ideas support the objective(s) of the meeting.

- Assist in the process of arriving at a consensus by combining ideas with those of others, reconciling them through compromise, or coordinating them with other ideas.
- Do away with non-relevant issues, perceptions, or personal conjectures as soon as they arise and before they can become disruptive.
- Always be patient and flexible (but with caution).

Major Problems in Running a Meeting

One of the major problems a group often faces at the beginning of a meeting is reaching agreement on both top-level and sub-level objectives. The objectives must be agreed upon before the meeting proceeds, if it is to be successful.

A second major problem concerns the personalities of participants. For example, the chairman may be dominant/submissive, have a desire to be liked, or want to impress his superiors. On the other hand, the invited participants may be self-centered, talkative/shy, aggressive/defensive, argumentative/unresponsive. The participants may have trouble communicating because of differences in age, rank, expertise, and prestige. The ideas of some participants may be ignored and others ridiculed. The mood of the group may be one of elation, depression, or regression.

There is no way to avoid these personality problems; therefore, the challenge facing the chairman is how to deal with them effectively. The answer is based upon creating an environment for effective communication. The problems can usually be resolved if the participants can communicate with one another. The problems will not be resolved if they remain hidden.

A firmly established, finite time limit for the meeting is the single most effective means of eliminating non-contributory discussion. It gives the group a common purpose and helps the chair- man police inappropriate comments.

Another major problem that groups sometimes face is having participants become lost in the problems they are attempting to solve. When this happens the chairman must take positive action to bring the meeting back on target. He can do this by taking one of the following two courses of action:

- Halting the discussion and redirecting the meeting.
- Halting the discussion and trying to find out where it is heading. If it is heading in a direction the participants feel is proper, he can allow the discussion to continue where it left off. If the meeting is heading in the wrong direction, he can change the direction.

The latter is preferable. Failure to do anything almost guarantees failure of the meeting. Halting the discussion and redirecting the meeting without providing an opportunity for participants to comment tends to create a debilitating emotional reaction. This might lead to withdrawal of some participants from further discussion, or precipitate aggression. When the participants pause to consider where the discussion is heading, there will be few adverse effects and the progress of the meeting may be enhanced.

A fourth major problem a group might face is how to make a decision at the proper time. If the chairman feels a consensus has been reached, he should cut off further discussion. A decision reached by consensus is the one most likely to be carried into action effectively. Decisions imposed on a minority by the majority of participants, or on the participants by the chairman, are not likely to be lasting or effective.

Groups often fall short in trying to reach decisions. Outside pressures or deadlines tend to foster majority-type or chairman-type decisions. Therefore, it is imperative that the chairman attempt to create an environment to make a consensus easier to obtain. Such an environment develops when each participant is given an opportunity to be heard or to voice an objection. In any case, before the meeting time limit expires the chairman should try to get the participants to agree that a decision is necessary, even if it falls short of unanimity.

Coping with Weakness

In order to make meetings more effective, one must be acquainted with the major weaknesses and ways to cope with them. The most common weaknesses of meetings are that they are slow, expensive, tend to produce a leveling effect, or lead to dilution or division of responsibility. Let's take a closer look at each of these weaknesses.

Meetings tend to be a slow way to get things done. They do not lend themselves to quick, decisive actions. One observer of committee meetings stated, "They keep minutes and waste hours." Delays are not always bad. Delays provide time for objective reviews or ideas and development and/or consideration of alternatives. Thus, delays can lead to better decisions. For a meeting to be effective, those with expertise and/or the need for action, should attend. Inviting experts and providing sufficient time to consider alternative solutions to problems increases the cost of a meeting. However, the cost to an organization if the meeting is not held may be far greater.

There is a tendency at meetings to bring the individual thinking of the participants in line with the average quality of the group's thinking. This leveling effect takes place when a participant begins to think less as an individual and adapts the ideas of other participants. The normal tendency is to accept ideas of the most dominant individual at the meeting although his ideas may not be the best. Leveling is not always undesirable; it tempers unreasonable ideas and curbs autocrats. The chairman should try to curb the leveling tendency. One way to keep a dominating participant in check is to seat him directly to the chairman's right.

The tendency for a decision made at a meeting to dilute or divide responsibility is a serious one. When this happens, weak managers are prone to blame their failures on that decision. Such comments as "I didn't support this approach at the meeting" are used to explain their failure to perform effectively. The chairman must be attuned to decisions that tend to dilute or divide responsibility and find a way to avoid them. All of the participants should be given an opportunity to express their viewpoints before the decision is made.

Wrap-up and Follow-up

The most important part of the meeting is its ending. After all information has been presented, all decisions made, all problem solutions found or all conclusions reached, the chairman must summarize and solidify the results. He must review decisions and then perceive any conflicts that might result. He must give those who made a major contribution to the meeting the credit they deserve. If no major decisions were reached, he must emphasize progress made and nail down assignments that will lead to a future decision-type meeting. The chairman must always follow through on his promises to the group; otherwise the participants will have no enthusiasm for participating in a future meeting if called upon to do so, If a meeting is a prologue to action, the epilogue must produce results. When no action follows a meeting, the meeting can be considered a failure. The chairman must never allow himself to think "activity" is the same as "accomplishment."

To translate decisions reached in a meeting into actions, the chairman must conduct the necessary follow-up action. A strategy used by successful chairmen is to:

- Plan the follow-up procedure before the meeting;
- Adjust the procedure during the meeting; and
- Consolidate the procedure after the meeting.

When the chairman follows up on meeting decisions, he demonstrates that meetings can accomplish something. This encourages future participation.

Summary

Meetings are an essential management tool. Meetings can improve communications, promote coordination, develop people, and help to get a job done. Poor meetings waste time and resources and discourage people. In preparing for a meeting, the chairman should ensure that the agenda focuses on accomplishment of specific objectives.

From time to time throughout the meeting, the chairman should take a census to determine whether the objectives are still valid. If not, they should be revised.

For a meeting to be successful, it must be supported within the organization and provide a needed decision or produce worthwhile actions. This will not occur unless several weaknesses related to meetings are overcome: their slowness, expense, tendency to create leveling, and tendency to dilute or divide responsibility.

Also, for a meeting to be successful, consideration must be given to the timing, meeting place, seating arrangements, size of room, and visual aids.

The leader of a meeting must have the right attitude; a well-conceived plan; and the ability to direct (focus), control, motivate, interpret, and moderate the meeting. He must recognize that reaching initial or revised objectives of the meeting, and follow-up after the meeting, are essential to its success.

The value of an effective meeting may be summed up as follows: It serves as the cornerstone for successful team-building and progress within an organization.

12. How To Get Organized

Achieving goals in an efficient way is possible when you know how to get organized. Here are some ideas and tips that will teach you how to get organized.

- Use an App that you carry with you at all times to help keep yourself organized.
- Use check lists and check sheets regularly for those things which must be done in a correct way.
- Have different-colored checklists for easy identification.
- When people come back to you asking the same question they have asked several times before, ask them to set up a standard operating procedure by simply writing down the statement that you are to make about how the situation is to be handled. They can then keep that at their desk, and will not have to ask you about it in the future.
- Create a visible time line for key projects.
- Make a daily "to-do" list of activities that you must do and set priorities on it every day. Then do the activities in priority order.
- Use a tickler or follow-up file allowing you to file items until the day that you can act on them.
- Set up a system to handle repetitive tasks.
- Avoid over organizing to the point where your perfectionism interferes with your achieving results.
- Identify and post reorder quantities on office supplies to prevent running out completely.

- Carry 3x5 cards or a notebook or note paper or your pocket calendar to make notes of things that you would like to remember.
- When doing work on a computer, have a regular routine of backing up your work at least twice a day to ensure it does not get lost.
- Dictate your notes or thoughts for projects on a cassette, then either have it transcribed by your secretary or personally pay a student to do it for you.
- Work on only one item at a time.
- Keep only one project on your desk at a time to avoid distractions. Time is lost sorting through other items while you're working on one.
- If you are working on several projects, keep each one in a clearly labeled file by itself so you do not have to look through a mixed project file to find things.
- Do not schedule every minute of the day; keep flexible for the unexpected items that will come up,
- When you sense things are out of control-STOP. Sit quietly, relax, re-establish priorities in writing, decide what action to take, then go again.
- Sit down and do all trivia in one sitting to get it over with.
- Build flexibility into your schedule by purposely overestimating the amount of time needed on each activity.
- Use a people page-a page that has an individual's name at the top on which you write down the routine things you want to ask this individual. Then call this person once a day, or at most, twice to ask all the questions that have accumulated on the page.

- If you are responsible for several key projects, use project pages in your calendar or planner. Keep one page on each project. Whenever you think of something that is relevant to that project, jot it down on the appropriate page. This way you will be organizing your thoughts as you have them.
- Schedule a meeting with yourself every day. Then during this meeting work uninterrupted on your top priority project.
- Carry a project with you so when kept waiting in a doctor's office, airport or on a bus, you can be productive.
- Before leaving the office at night, put the most important project for tomorrow on your desk. It will be there ready and waiting for you in the morning.
- Establish an efficient working routine that matches you and your job. Do a certain activity at the same time each day or on the same day every week.
- Organize items you reference frequently in a ring binder in protective plastic. It will enhance its usability and present ability to customers or to yourself.
- Keep a log of requests made. Be sure to note the day and hour they are to be completed.
- Each day make a Call-See-Do list. Who you should call. Who you should see, and what you should do.
- Consolidate support staff where possible. For example, typing staff could be reorganized into a pool to equalize their work loads.
- Create specific useful forms such as time sheets and other record keeping sheets that are helpful to a specific job, but do not bog down the people with redundant paperwork.

- Keep only one calendar and keep it with you at all times.
- Combine all personal and work related items into your one personal calendar.
- Gather all needed materials and supplies for a project. Then when you sit and do the project, you won't have to run for this item or that item.
- Capture a few minutes from every activity you do. They accumulate to be extra time for your high priority projects.
- Use the computer where practical for reports and processing of information gathered.
- Instead of using a standard form it may pay off to make a customized form for a special customer. Assess the situation carefully.
- Trade days. Work on Saturday when it is quiet and take another day or two half days off.
- Implement flex time to help employee motivation.
- Once you are sure you are doing the most important thing, then ask yourself: "How can I do this more efficiently?"
- Use short, simple, written directions for routine procedures.
- Move your in-basket off the desk so it will not be a temptation or distraction.
- As things you must do come to mind, write them down in your pocket planner or calendar immediately so they do not get lost.
- Look for ways of automating office procedures.
- Work four 10-hour days instead of five 8-hour days. It gives you an extra day at home and better concentration at work.

- Use a steno pad to list thoughts, duties, interruptions or questions. Use a highlighter to cross them off as you deal with them.
- Keep a notebook with pages headed "Thanks giving,"
- "Christmas," "Office party," or the name of other special projects. Then when you think of something that must be done or bought, etc., you can jot it down on the appropriate page.
- Make up daily/weekly/monthly/quarterly lists of routine duties with blank spaces to fill in responsibilities and special duties.
- Group like tasks together to prevent job jumping and wasting time.
- Provide adequate private work space as well as central areas and conference space to maximize effectiveness.
- Buy ahead so you have supplies on hand.
- Ask people who are not closely involved with a problem or process how they think it could be done. You will get fresh ideas.
- Use the proper tools for the job even if you have to go out and purchase them.
- Develop personal systems that work for you, then follow them. Be sure to update them periodically.
- At night put classified material in a secure place. Do not leave it out where it might walk off.
- Clean your desk the last five minutes of the day and prepare it for getting started first thing in the morning.
- Keep papers you are not working on in the filing cabinet, not on your desk.
- Keep supplies and materials in a storage cabinet, not on your desk.

- Establish an organized filing system that anyone can use and see that things get into it immediately.
- Save simplistic, repetitious, routine, manual jobs, (folding papers, stuffing envelopes) for times when you choose to simply relax and chat with others, or listen to cassette tapes.
- List key activities on 3x5 cards, one to a card. Review them in priority sequence several times each day.
- Stick "Post-It-Notes" on projects to show status or progress of a project.
- Role model as an organized person. You will soon convince yourself.
- Devise a problem resolution log which keeps track of progress on solving problems within a department.
- Schedule a block of time to be dedicated to major projects.
- When you think other people might forget something important, use multiple reminders to jog their memory. Use such things as notes, lists, tickler reports, status reports, briefings, phone calls, special bulletins, and so forth.
- Look for two or more complementary activities that can be dovetailed and done at one time.
- When you receive a person's business card, write notes about your encounter on the back of the card.

13. How to Improve Your Planning Skills

Planning skills is written about and talked about more than it is done. Here are some ideas that will help you improve your planning skills and planning ability.

- Force yourself to plan.
- If you fail to plan, you are by default planning to fail.
- Schedule uninterrupted time every day to do your planning.
- Anticipate possible problems you could encounter in your project because of people, material, or mechanical failures. Purposely provide preventive actions and contingency plans in important high risk situations.
- When planing a project, plan in thinking time.
- Plan for tomorrow, tonight. Your subconscious will help organize while you sleep.
- Each day anticipate the sequence of activities that you will do to attain the objectives you are after.
- Think about your entire week. How will important projects be sequenced?
- Do your planning on paper to capture all of your ideas and to be sure none of them get lost. We can only work mentally with about seven pieces of information without losing some- thing. Write your thoughts down and you will be able to utilize everything you think of during your planning process.

- When developing a specific plan, list the activity steps individually on small pieces of paper and then sequence the pieces of paper. Then write the whole plan out in sequential order.
- If you must, leave your office and get away to do your planning in a quiet place where you can think.
- Don't hurry the process. Something will get overlooked.

- When things go wrong, it can generally be traced back to a poor job of planing or failing to follow an existing plan.
- List key words that relate to a project. They will fit into and help you in planning. Keep records of how long it takes to do an activity. You can use this information for future scheduling.
- Take the first 10'&127;6 of any time block and dedicate it to planning that block.
- Whether you call it planning time, thinking time, quiet time or meditation, the payoff in increased productivity is the same.
- Schedule one weekend away each quarter and make it a top priority. Mini-vacations are refreshing.
- Encourage your staff to create their own plan and then to explain it in detail to you.
- Sit quietly and mentally rehearse the steps in your plan. Use your imagination to visualize the steps being taken. You will sense where additional steps need to be added and will anticipate problems to prevent.
- Consider settling for 90% completion of 90% of the projects. The final 10% may not be worth the cost to attain them.

- Use the first 10 minutes of each day to plan or review your plan for the day.
- When starting a new project or activity, take a moment to quietly review, mentally, the steps you will follow.
- Set your own due dates for projects earlier than the actual deadline.
- Put schedules in writing. Publish them and then follow up with them.
- If you cannot identify the objectives and steps to take to get to a goal, it is "unrealistic."
- Mentally organize before proceeding.
- Create and use Gantt charts.
- Create and use PERT charts.
- Stick Post-It-Notes on paperwork to indicate or highlight scheduling and due dates.
- Remember the 6 P's of planning: Proper Prior Planning Prevents Poor Performance.
- Schedule formal planning meetings with your staff regularly.

14. How To Better Manage Yourself

You are responsible for everything that happens in your life. Learn to accept total responsibility for yourself. If you do not manage yourself, then you are letting others have control of your life. These self management tips will help "you" manage "you."

- Look at every new opportunity as an exciting and new-life experience.
- If you catch yourself worrying about an upcoming task, go ahead and do it now so it no longer is a distraction.
- Get into the habit of finishing what you start.
- Give up "waiting time" forever. Have something with you at all times to work on. For example: plan your day, work on a report, or read a page from your book.
- Be a professional who exhibits self-confidence and self-assurance in your potential to complete any task.
- Avoid worry. The majority of the things you worry about never occur.
- Agree with yourself in advance that you will have a good attitude toward the upcoming task.
- Hire specialists to do those things you are not expert in.
- Take a chance-calculated risks pay off in entrepreneurial progress.
- Frequently ask, "Is what I am doing right now moving me toward my goals?"

- Plan the future, but live in the present.

- Make a list of your accomplishments as you go through the day-they are greater than you think.
- Keep a time log at least once every six months to determine exactly where your time is going.
- Do it right the first time and you will not have to take time later to fix it.
- Practice concentrating on your work, doing only one thing at a time.
- Accept responsibility for your job successes and failures. Do not look for a scapegoat.
- Do not view things you do as a "job." View all activities as a challenge.
- Use your subconscious mind by telling it to do what you do want. Instead of telling yourself, "I can't do that very well," say, "I can do this very well."
- Schedule several short vacations or long weekends-this creates positive deadlines by when you must have projects done.
- Develop a faster operating tempo or pace. Do things with a sense of urgency. Get over thinking you must do everything yourself.
- Take time to be quiet and reflective for a few minutes each day.
- Live effectiveness in everything you do rather then just sporadically applying time management techniques.
- Live in the Now. The current instant is the only time in which you have control-not the past, not the future, just now, in this instant.
- Recognize you control only 50% of a relationship and that is your half. If you are dissatisfied with what is going on, change what you are doing and saying.

- Give yourself points for completing tasks on your "to-do" list in priority order. When you reach 10 points, reward yourself.
- Carry a card with your goals written on it and review your goals at least three times a day.
- Act with enthusiasm in all that you do.
- Take time out to thank yourself for a good job.
- Practice your personal beliefs. It may be helpful each morning to take 15 minutes to gather your thoughts and say a prayer.
- Operate knowing that there is good in everything. Every cloud has a silver lining-look for it.
- Whenever you have an important thought that is not directly related to what you are working on, write it down. Then you will not forget it and you also will no longer be distracted by it.
- Make a commitment to show someone a specific accomplishment on a certain date. The added urgency will help you feel motivated to have it done.
- Reward yourself when you have successfully completed a high priority project.
- Instead of thinking about what you didn't get done, recognize all you did get accomplished and reward yourself for having done the most important things.
- Keep a list of accomplishments as well as a list of "things to-do. You will learn just how much you do get done.
- Practice self determination, wanting to do it for yourself.
- Nothing takes the place of persistence. Practice "stick-to-it-iveness."
- Get into the habit of writing down a person's name-it will help you to remember it.
- Believe that you can be what you want to he.

- Operate on the philosophy that what we give out is what comes back to us.
- Occasionally, sit quietly and do a self-assessment of your skills and strengths.
- Praise yourself for your progress.
- Recognize not all days will go as you desire. Be kind to yourself on days when your self esteem is wavering. Remind yourself that you are good and can stand up to any obstacle.
- Never criticize yourself as having a weakness. There is no such thing. You are only talking about a present undeveloped skill or part of yourself that if you so chose, you can change. You do not have any weakness, only untapped potential.
- Check to be sure you do not fall into the activity trap of simply doing tasks without knowing to what greater good the task is designed to contribute.
- Be pleasant all the time-no matter what the situation.
- Life is what you perceive it to be. Do you see it as a bore or as an adventure?
- Recall what you were hired to do and make sure it happens.
- To get ahead in anything, operate in the "and then some" manner. Always do what is expected "and then some," so what you give is always more than is expected by the other person.
- When working on a project that you can't stand, do it for a few minutes at a time until you can't stand it anymore. Then do something else and come back later for a few more minutes. Keep taking these bite size pieces until it is completely done.
- Look at what you do as an adventure. You can discover new things from this new perspective.

- Challenge yourself to do things differently than you have in the past. It provides new ideas and keeps you interested.
- Finish that last task you are working on before you go home; do not just leave it.
- Plan your day as you shower and dress in the morning. Keep a pad and pencil nearby to jot down ideas.
- Talk to yourself. Self talk using positive affirmations is something that is common among all great achievers. They convince themselves that they can accomplish their goals.
- Practice being punctual. Others will sense your professionalism.
- Plan, at least to a minimum, everything you undertake.
- Think it through, then do it.
- Think of your time as money. Are you getting a good return on the way you invest/spend it?
- Take some time, no matter how short, every day to do something you enjoy.
- Remember, if you think you can or you think you cannot, you are right.
- Use the self-fulfilling prophesy on yourself. Expect yourself to succeed.
- Doing gives you the power to do.
- Whenever you agree to get back to someone or complete a project, commit to a specific date by when you will have it done. and write this in your calendar immediately.
- Think in terms of long-term results.
- Create your own "motivation board" by putting up notes of things you need to do on a bulletin board or special wall space. It is an easily visible way to see

what you need to work on. When an item is done, remove the note. Also keep your goals listed and pictured on your board.

- "Ninety percent of success in showing up."
- Be open and ready to make adjustments as things change.
- Focus 100% of your attention on a project.
- Since your boss will be asking you for progress reports, from time to time, stay informed by asking your people for progress reports each day while you meet them in their office or work area.
- Hire an assistant to run small errands and cleanup paperwork, etc. Even if you pay them from your own pocket, it is a good investment because it increases your productivity.
- Enjoy your life and blessings. You could be worse off.
- Recognize that even though you say you are doing something for someone else, in reality you are doing it for yourself. Since you are doing it for yourself, you can also enjoy it more.
- Start each day with a smile.
- Your job reflects you. Can you take pride in it being well done, error free and on time?
- Do it right or do it wrong just do it!
- Compete with yourself to become a little better each time you do something. Achieve your potential.
- Streamline your daily routine to do the same thing at the same time in the same order. Periodically review for continued effectiveness and efficiently.
- When responsible for a project, become intensively involved with it.
- Tell someone else what you are doing to keep on schedule. It keeps you committed.

- Make each day the best day of the week.
- Network with others in the organization to stay informed of who is doing what, when, where, and for whom.
- Use even small "pockets of time" to make lists, write notes and consider ideas.
- Consciously decide what are some things you are NOT going to do.
- Be willing to ask that a staff meeting be called to clarify a specific issue.
- Purposely schedule something you enjoy between routine projects. It will help rejuvenate you.
- Schedule a block of time periodically to take a big bite out of a major project.
- Realize "energy begets energy." Act and energy will flow.
- Time your routine activities such as telephone calls. Determine how you can "capture" some of the time and use it on other top priority activities.
- Be a "doer" not a "sitter."
- Sense the pride you will feel when you have completed a project.
- "He who kills time buries opportunities."
- Meditate according to your personal beliefs at the beginning of each day.
- Create the right "mind set" for success by adjusting your attitude for the upcoming project.
- Stay interested in what you are doing. Keep looking for what is interesting in your work. Change your perspective and look at it as someone outside your job would,
- Do not get hung-up on trivial details or tangents. Stay focused and moving.

- Always carry a pen or pencil and paper on which you can make notes.
- Do not accept calls for the first 15 minutes of the day while you prepare your daily strategy.
- Contemplating, meditating on, thinking about, or praying about the activities and success of the workday focuses energy toward that end result.
- Nest activities to available waiting time. Take a bite out of your elephant-sized project.
- Establish personal incentives and rewards to help maintain your own high enthusiasm and performance level.

Made in the USA
San Bernardino, CA
13 February 2018